UNCOVERING AUTISM

A BOOK OF POETRY

Matthew Ansell

First published in 2018 by Paragon Publishing, Rothersthorpe
© Matthew Ansell 2018

ISBN 978-1-78222-642-0

Book design, layout and production management by Into Print
www.intoprint.net
+44 (0)1604 832149

FOREWORD

The author of this book of poetry, Matthew Ansell, had Asperger's Syndrome (AS) from his birth in 1972. This is a condition on the autistic spectrum. However, knowledge and understanding of this condition was very limited, even among professionals in this field. He was not officially diagnosed until the age of about 28 after attending a London psychiatric hospital for a series of tests. He later went on to assist them into research of this condition as a volunteer.

AS is sometimes known as the invisible disability. This is because at first glance most people with this condition look absolutely normal. One would think that this is a good thing but it does have its disadvantages. Often it is not until you spend, even a little time with someone with this disability, that you come to realise that their behaviour is unusual. One of the many symptoms of AS is the problems sufferers have with social interaction. They often do not interact well with others, being unable to contribute to conversations and being unable to read body-language. They can be unkindly thought of as weird. Consequently they are not given the consideration and understanding they need. Indeed they are sometimes ridiculed or bullied.

Most people who have not come into contact with someone with AS have little idea how difficult life can be for them. Coping with the world around them is a daily struggle. They have to try so much harder to achieve things that most people would find quite easy.

Matthew created this collection of poetry in his 20s as a means of communicating his emotions and problems over the years of his childhood and early adulthood. This collection of poetry may help parents and others to understand what it is like to have this condition. Additionally perhaps, giving fellow sufferers some encouragement when they realise that the situations and feelings described in these verses may mirror their own.

PJA

Illustrations

Other than *Button Love* and the painting *Poppy Garden* all of the colour illustrations in this book, including the front cover, are pictures of mosaics designed by the author and created from hundreds of individual pieces of coloured card.

A portrait of the author Matthew Ansell,
aged about 8 years, drawn by his cousin
Vanessa.

Contents

Star Burst

Life Through a Prism

How can I define autism?
Like looking at life through a prism
So many different colours
With light and dark shades; each ray dispersed.

There is no clear edge to divide
The colours, though I certainly tried
It was a task too great for me
Yet all the shades did seem to agree.

I don't know where I fit in this
Should I try too hard or just dismiss?
Is colour real just because we
Have magical vision so we can see?

I cannot feel the sensations
For colour has just got no patience
It's just a blur; complicated
Everything's destroyed, and created.

Dedicated to Autism Awareness Week

Autism is not just a state of mind
Unfair to say it cannot be defined
Try to listen to us, then you might hear
In all we do an element of fear
Striving to function in a normal way
Much of life not black and white
                              but shades of grey.

Although we may sometimes appear to be
Weird in our approach to things; but you see
Autistic people have to learn those skills
Real life means you have to climb many hills
Every day there's a new challenge ahead
Never underestimate what we dread
Each obstacle brings fear, a racing heart
Sometimes we really don't know where to start,
So please be aware of Autism Awareness.

The Sea of Chaos

Lost in a sea of chaos
When sights and sounds don't matter
Slightest things will make me cross
And broken dreams will shatter.

Sight of losing precious time
When all around is ageing
Doing nothing is a crime
The sea of chaos raging.

How can I change the present?
By looking to the future?
Surely what was ever meant
Is the same as was before.

The tempest of stormy days
Will oceans ever be calm
As stillness precedes sun rays
No more will I come to harm.

Finding my Place

How can I find my place
Amongst the human race
When I just don't fit in
And turmoil's felt within.

What crazy world is this
Where so much goes amiss
I can't make any sense
For life is too intense.

Where no-one understands
And all just make demands
My head wants to explode
I just can't crack the code!

A simple life I yearn
Without such great concern
A quiet existence
If I could have the chance.

Body-Language

Body-language may seem simple to you
But if you ask me; I haven't a clue
Mannerisms and facial expressions
To unravel this, I need some lessons.

What comes naturally to you may seem
Unreal; but to me it's just a bad dream
How can I possibly make sense of some
Unspoken language; then I'm standing dumb.

If I offend you with a silent voice
Or if I say something and it annoys
Please understand this is a common theme
And sometimes it leaves me wanting to scream.

Maybe people like me should learn to sign
And then perhaps I would get on just fine
For an impairment it is, no-one sees
But sometimes when standing there; I freeze.

Misunderstood

The autistic boy walks down the street
Everyone staring whom he should meet
Some of the children laugh, for they know
This is the boy; a little bit slow.

His appearance and dress sense seem quite odd
He ignores them when they poke and prod
He runs away down adjoining roads
Away from the taunting and constant goads.

They do not know how he feels inside
At least he can hold his head with pride
He knows he is brainier by far
So he just follows his promised star.

A Is for Autism

A is for autism; misunderstood
When we can't do all the things that we should
How do you explain to a passer-by
Why your child suddenly lets out a cry.

The glares and the comments, nobody knows
The world we live in; eternally closed
How you wish that you could be miles away
That your child would learn how normal kids play.

You know that they can't help the way they are
But how do you cope with this constant war
When nothing seems to work and all seems lost
The waves of life being forever tossed.

Communication which can't be expressed
When isolation seems surely the best
How do you tell which route to be taking
And what is left that can be forsaken.

Time and support are all that you can give
The greatest tools which will help us to live
For time is a healer and a great friend
And support brings out the best in the end.

Life In a Prison Cell

Life in a prison cell
Great clanging iron-doors
Caused by internal hell
As fighting for the cause.

Drowning in the sorrow
Words cannot be expressed
Hoping for tomorrow
When the torment can rest.

Will the chains be released
Will the shutters open
Will the battle have ceased
And normal life begin.

Will there be much wailing
Alone in the prison
Thoughts of dread they bring
To live with autism.

Acceptance

I just ask you to accept me
The way that I am; for I know
There are things that I do not see
And places I struggle to go.

All I want is to know you care
That you won't leave me when I fail
And someone with whom I can share
Life's storms together we can sail.

The passion of love transcending
Making me whole, ever reaching
This pure magic, never-ending
More wonderful than anything.

I see the truth and shed a tear
As I try to quench the burning fire
I see no hope within my fear
There goes my pain; full of desire.

What Is…?

What is play?
A crazy day
What are friends?
That life depends.

What is speech?
Some words for each
What is care
Something we share.

Tongue-Tied

How do you chat up a girl?
What do you say to attract?
Must you go through constant hell?
Or do you put on an act?

What happens if you are shy?
Are there any solutions?
I'd rather curl up and die
Than cause all these confusions.

I'm usually tongue-tied
And can't think of the right words
So I tend to run and hide
And hope nobody observes.

Heart-ache is like burning fire
Rejection scars you so deep
This is the power of desire
Which can turn me to a heap.

Am I meant to be psychic
How should I know what to say?
Do people suddenly click
Not black and white, but just grey.

It Means Nothing

I don't know what you are thinking
Do you know what is on my mind?
Are you mentally linking
Is that the way brains were designed?

I really don't know the answer
I don't have the understanding
To make any response occur
And I just find that I'm sinking.

Should I know how you are feeling
Before you have verbally said
There is no way of revealing
By using other means instead.

I cannot connect with you this way
It means nothing every silence
Why don't you just speak out and say
Rather than build up your defence.

No Rules for Love

There are no rules; this is the plight
I wrestle with this day and night
The urge to overcome and find
That which to me is not aligned.

Frustration overwhelms me so
And though this does not outward show
Inside a battle has commenced
I feel totally inward fenced.

Questions forever come to mind
Was I just not for love designed?
Always alone; will I be left
Would my hope be ever bereft?

A missing piece from the jigsaw
A tender heart that feels so raw
Truth of love will I ever know
At dusk; the sun is ever low.

Button Love

The Patch

I had a friend when I was young
He was a fairly normal chap
A bag across his back was slung
And he usually wore a cap.

His clothing scruffy; so modest
And his appearance quite unkempt
I'm sure his shirt was never pressed
And with his hair made no attempt.

Though he did not really stand out
In a crowd for his appearance
But one thing without any doubt
Made his personal difference.

People used to stand, start to stare
I thought this was terribly rude
Wherever we went, everywhere
I could feel that their eyes were glued.

The reason; my friend wore a patch
Constantly was on his left eye
Though he still could bowl; also catch
He could do it better than I.

I just don't know what he had wrong
It did make him look slightly odd
But I didn't notice for long
And many paths since; we have trod.

25

I Knew I Could Do It

I knew I could do it
But nobody believed
They thought I was half-wit
And my heart was aggrieved.

For a time this made me
Sit back and do nothing
Through this; all I could see
I had to do something.

Sure, it was hard at first
But I knew it was right
And at the very worst
It could fail; it just might!!

I had to take the chance
Something had to be done
Someone had to advance
The risk; I had to run.

The moral of all this
If something must be done
It's best not to dismiss
But to be that "someone"!!

Learning to Ride

I learnt to ride a bicycle when I was ten years old
It felt like I had won a medal for Olympic Gold
For the trials and frustrations that I had had to endure
Whilst practising co-ordination like never before.

More than once I fell off and received the odd bump and
bruise
Which knocked my confidence but I tried not to get the blues
I just got back up on my bicycle and pedalled slow
Until I felt again that my confidence began to grow.

I never understood why it took me so long to learn
Though I tried not to show my anxiety and concern
I knew that it would take me longer than my other peers
So I strived and battled onwards; through all the trials and tears.

The day that I succeeded and rode my bike around the block
I was overcome with elation; time stopped on the clock
The tears that followed would be tears of joy not sorrow
And the pride that I felt inside would make my heart glow.

Safe In my Thoughts

All alone in my thoughts
I'm quietly thinking
No interest in sports
Contact games; team linking.

They are there, I am here
I just don't want to know
Quick movements make me fear
I'd rather slowly go.

Much yelling and shouting
Pure squeals of excitement
It just has me writhing
I need enlightenment.

Seems to be no structure
Nor are there any rules
Like uncivilised war
No guns; but bats and balls.

The Importance of Play

They expected me to go and play
With other children in the street
But there were no rules; to my dismay
So I just stared down at my feet.

I knew they were cross, but knew not why
Why was play-time so important
I didn't get anywhere though I tried
Yet everyone seemed defiant.

The teachers said that I must join in
My parents ever had pursued
To make me play – my head's in a spin
This was something I could not do.

The guilt that I felt sure knew no bounds
I knew that I was different
Just from the looks and many frowns
But that was quite irrelevant.

Hidden Messages

How do I know that you like me?
How do you know that I like you?
Questions like these are not easy
Do you find them difficult too?

How should you tell someone that you
Like them? What words should you use
And why is it so hard to do
For words often hurt and abuse.

Can you read how someone's feeling?
Is it a look or expression?
Can you tell what they're concealing
Or do you get an impression?

Is it their tone of voice; inflexions?
Are there hidden messages too?
I find many complications
Which leave me with hardly a clue.

Sounds and Vibrations

Sounds and vibrations entered my head
The most powerful noises I knew
These were the moments which I would dread
Fear took hold; I knew not what to do.

The sensitivity in my ears
Would raise an alarm very quickly
Which would soon have me break down in tears
And it then made me feel quite sickly.

I'd bury my head into my lap
Close my eyes so that I could not see
This monster which would lay me a trap
For a prisoner then I would be.

The sheer volume of sound made me reel
Even as I was getting older
For I knew that my senses could feel
Sometimes sharper and that much bolder.

Menacing

I don't get it
Why do they stare?
Wish they would quit
This I can't bear.

I'm just the same
But I am not!
This is a game
It gets too hot.

I hear them laugh
Loud with malice
They cross my path
It's so callous!

Why should I move?
I was here first
What would it prove?
I watch them disperse.

Heightened Awareness

Thinking in pictures
Head full of mixtures
Can't focus clearly
No-one can hear me.

Many new faces
People and places
All in a muddle
Sat in a huddle.

The image too bright
I can't see the light
The noise is too loud
I hear in the crowd.

Sensations I feel
It is a big deal
Heightened awareness
Causes me much stress.

Sometimes I must go
To somewhere I know
Where I feel comfort
Some place I have sought.

The Logical Solution

The logical solution
Would avoid much confusion
I like it plain and easy
Otherwise it would tease me.

Don't think I'm being awkward
But I just find it too hard
To take in too many rules
Long equations and symbols.

Please get back to the basics
Then we might have some success
It needs to be black or white
Or else I will just take flight.

There are many routes to take
But keep it clear for my sake
Else my brain just won't take in
This code that we are breaking!

Transformation

It seems so wrong to think this way
Why can't I see you as a friend
For that's how it was yesterday
And I sure don't want it to end.

For you have not changed overnight
And I am still me; that I know
And these feelings just don't seem right
With my heart beating fast and slow.

If neither of us have changed then
Why can't I continue the way
That we were, good friends; so open
Yet now we have a price to pay.

This transformation so quickly
How do I deal with emotions
For it makes me feel so sickly
And causes many commotions.

Caught In a Bubble

Caught in a bubble
Swept up in the sky
Whisked at the double
As I learn to fly.

How I now look down
And see far below
The streets and the town
And people I know.

How did I get here?
What do I do next?
With hope and much fear
That's what they expect.

Where am I going?
And when do I stop?
Do I keep growing
Or do I just drop?

Trusting

Trusting – I was never in doubt
Thought I knew what they were about
Whatever was said I believed
How many times was I deceived?

Assuming that they were honest
I would surely never have guessed
People could tell so many lies
So it came as a big surprise.

Did I wake one day knowing the truth?
I still felt there must be some proof
I smelt fear; foundations were gone
Building blocks I built my life upon.

I had been naïve for so long
And yet; it still did not feel wrong
Those years of innocent acceptance
Which helped me to keep a distance.

Making my Mind Up

Shut in a cage
Built up with rage
Turn the next page
For my next stage.

Scared to proceed
What will life lead
What do I need
Now I am freed.

What do I choose
Are there no clues
No subtle cues
I feel the blues.

Time makes me wait
What is my fate
This I do hate
Work up a state.

Fear of the Unknown

Fear of the unknown
I feel so alone
What should I expect
What do I detect?

Too much to take in
My head's in a spin
I cannot focus
But I know I must.

Why is it so hard
Always on my guard
And in reflection
What's my impression?

How to face the dread
Should I stay in bed?
Easier option
Without disruption.

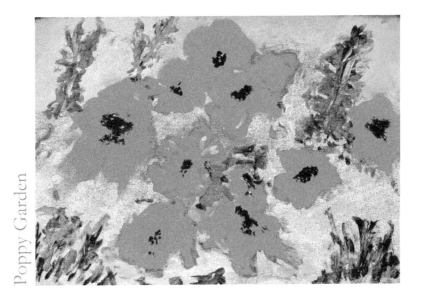

The Playground

I can't stand it
There's too much noise
I might get hit
By one of the boys.

In the playground
Movements so quick
My head feels drowned
It makes me quite sick.

If they come near
I know I'll hide
This constant fear
Cannot be denied.

They must not know
What I am feeling
I want to go
My head is reeling.

Too Many Faces

Too many faces stare at me
It makes me cringe and shake with fear
What do they expect me to be
I really don't want to be here.

I don't know why I had to come
For I find that these occasions
Normally make me feel struck dumb
And I can't make conversations.

They tell me that I must come though
For it is expected of me
I really loathe it when we go
Mixing with friends and family.

They never will understand why
I hate to go to these events
And I must admit that I try
Though the struggle makes me feel tense.

Life for the Autistic

Life for the autistic
Needs to be simplistic
With regular routines
Not constant changing scenes.

The patterns unbroken
Speech that must be spoken
No interferences
Change and differences.

Precise to the minute
Not perfect? Then bin it
And must be achieving
Or else comes the grieving.

Giving up won't exist
When we're 'lost in the mist'
We'd rather keep trying
And failure denying.

Systems Are Slow

Systems are slow
Where do I go?
No one does know
How can I grow?

Disillusion
Much confusion
Caused dysfunction
Not construction.

Answers don't come
Makes me feel glum
I am struck dumb
Caught in this scrum.

War in my head
Weighed down like lead
This do I dread
I leave instead.

The Next Bell

I used to hide in the playground
Wondering if I would be found
Even after the bell had rung
I just stayed put and held my tongue.

Sometimes no one seemed to miss me
And I would think this a pity
For the concealment seemed pointless
But I remained nevertheless.

I missed many a lesson too
I'm glad that my mum never knew
She would have been mad that's for sure
And I would know what was in store.

When the next bell had rung for lunch
I started to have a slight hunch
No one wanted to look for me
Should I wait for the bell at three?

Better Than Expected

Don't ask me to explain
That makes me go insane
For it is a real pain
When you're left in the slow lane.

Don't ask for a reason
When everything goes wrong
For all that has been done
I don't find that much fun.

It's just this condition
And it is my mission
To have an ambition
To use my intuition.

The brain is affected
But I'm not defected
No one has detected
It's better than expected!

Struck Dumb

I am numb
Have been struck dumb
To this I succumb
Like the beat of a drum.

I hear noise
In the street, boys
Anxiously I poise
My shattered peace destroys.

I hear sound
Makes my heart pound
Coming from the ground
I feel as if I've drowned.

I'm alone
No one had known
Never had I shown
Such confidence; my own.

Hiding Places

One day in school I decide
That I was going to hide
So at play-time I went out
Into the field; round about.

I found some thick bushes there
That sprawled about everywhere
I stood close behind to see
If anyone followed me.

My plan had worked up till then
But being in the open
It had decided to rain
Should I go now or remain?

There's no fun in getting damp
I felt I was getting cramp
So I went back inside school
And then I nearly lost my cool.

Dare to be Different

Dare to be different
How and to what extent
Does it really matter
Will my whole world shatter.

Dare to be challenging
Are we not managing
Take nothing for granted
Is life so enchanted.

Dare to be ambitious
I find this delicious
Life is full of colour
I will live mine fuller.

And dare to be a voice
For those who have no choice
Those unable to speak
To help is what I seek.

Textures

Textures and fibres I've enjoyed
I love to touch; they feel so good
Though some people might get annoyed
But this I've never understood.

Playing with an elastic band
Stretching and pulling many ways
Fingers enjoying sifting sand
On the beach, many happy days.

Make sandcastles; watch them harden
As I put sand in my bucket
Blowing bubbles in the garden
Must blow the mixture; not suck it.

Watching them fly high in the air
What is the largest I can make
They seem to scatter everywhere
Then pop; the bubbles I forsake.

Underwater Scene

When Senses Are Heightened

When senses are heightened and awareness made greater
What pain we can feel when trying to co-operate
The powers we are given can be our worst traitor
For they work overtime; and that is to understate!

Thought processes which inhabit our minds can be cruel
Nervous energy takes over – then what do you do?
The wars within your brain are playing a constant duel
You are trying to fix together each little clue.

Powerful explosions taking place every second
Trying to decipher what is known to common man
Communicating silently when you are beckoned
How do I possibly fit in to this eternal plan?

Is there chance that my strengths compliment my weaknesses
Or that my weaknesses could be complicated too
For if I remains silent when all else expresses
Would this indicate to me what is I have to do?

Mind Games

Deep in the darkness
My head's in a mess
Utter confusion
Caused by delusion.

The sorrow I feel
I hope it will heal
I cannot control
This great gaping hole.

No light can pierce in
Will I ever win?
I am overcome
My head just feels numb.

Inside I'm crying
My heart is sighing
It wants to get out
From worse fear throughout.

Code-breaking

Life is a code that I can't crack
For I just do not have the knack
And rule books are not provided
By circumstance I'm guided.

It causes confusion I know
And frustration begins to grow
Uncommon language is relayed
Between others; but I have strayed.

Like a sentence without the words
Like halves broken down into thirds
How must I contemplate all this?
When everything has gone amiss.

Don't ask where it is I should go
For this feeling fills me with woe
That I make unknowing mistakes
Please let me know when the code breaks.

Code-breaking

People as Strangers

People are strangers everywhere
As I stand still, and stop and stare
Am I afraid of what they might do
And are they afraid of me too?

In terror I grab hold of my mum
She can see that I am struck dumb
Which is strange, I normally shout
There's something wrong with me, no doubt!

I would not go out on my own
Walking along the street alone
Afraid that someone might stop me
Wanting to talk, such agony!

I freeze at the thought that they might
Speak t o me; what an awful fright
I stay indoors till mum goes out
And then I follow her about.

The Perils of School

I didn't really want to go to school
Not in the early days anyway
Apart from feeling excluded from all
I would be alone, that was my way.

It wasn't that I didn't like learning
Nothing could be further from the truth
It was friendship that I was yearning
But I was a solitary youth.

I did not know that I needed a friend
I did not realise what friends do
This was something I could not comprehend
It was alien to me, so new.

School was too noisy and crowded I found
I could not concentrate very long
Especially hated the playground
Too much bustle, pushing along.

Again it was fear that smelt just so strong
Even I could not understand
Nobody could sense there was something wrong
And no one could ever have explained.

Learning to Read

I learnt to read when I was eight
I know that this was rather late
But though it was quite a slow start
I got it off to a fine art.

Always had a book in my hand
Broadened knowledge, mind to expand
Learnt to spell quickly, overtook
And nothing would I overlook.

Whilst others were still struggling
I was no longer worrying
I had raced ahead and was proud
For once I was in front of the crowd!

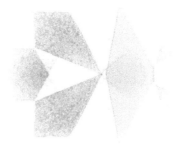

Lost In the System

We get lost in the system
Known as the difficult ones
We are seen as a problem
And we make complications.

What hope is there left for us?
We say nothing – they don't know
We say something, and that's a fuss
Progress made is very slow.

How many doors have been closed
How many sighs and head shakes
For when the truth is exposed
This system suddenly breaks.

A difference I could make
However small it may be
For mine and for others' sake
Smooth out the path, hopefully.

A Few Thoughts

Is it me or the rest of the world
That has gone totally mad
When the truth is finally unfurled
I shall be awfully glad.

What is it that really makes us tick
What's happening to our lives
And why does time have to pass so quick
So much enjoyment deprives.

Why do we dwell so much on the future
What's special about the past
Surely we should stop here and nurture
The present – how long does it last.

Why do others control our feelings
Our moods on daily bases
With many folk we have dealings
Too many frowning faces.

The Brick

Not out of my sight
Could it take flight
It was kept near
I held it dear.

Just a plastic brick
No special trick
It made me feel good
No-one understood.

I took it to school
When I was small
I waved it around
Whilst others frowned.

It was my comfort
That's what I thought
And when I felt sick
I just had my brick.

My World of Imagination

My world of imagination
That gives me much fascination
And can cause some complication
Yet I just feel the elation.

A world without walls or fences
Emotions heightened and senses
No problem with differences
No poverty; no expenses.

A world where all are respected
Where no ideals are expected
No-one considered defected
No malice has been detected.

A world full of many spaces
Takes you to wonderful places
With harmony amongst races
Many happy; smiling faces.

Staircase to Dreams

Always on the Move

Always on the move
Forever travelling
We don't get stuck in a groove
Time is unravelling.

Where is the destination
And where are we going
Passing through every station
We are never slowing.

How will we know when we reach
The place we are heading
That must be worked out by each
These webs need unthreading.

The journey can be tiring
Many knocks on the way
For what are we desiring
To get out of the fray!

Running With the Clock

Time is running out fast
Don't mourn then what is past
As I am standing still
But how can I fulfil?

Make use of what is left
Or else I'll feel bereft
Constant work all day long
This is where I belong.

The grief I feel inside
For time has got no pride
I run but it's no good
The clock won't slow; it should.

The sun rises and sets
The clock aids and abets
Maybe I should take stock
Stop running with the clock!

The Missing Piece

Digesting facts and figures
Whilst everyone else sniggers
What is considered normal
Rigid and uniformal?

Memory is fanatic
Not a hoax or just a trick
What you see is what you get
I owe no-one any debt.

The missing piece always there
You may say life is unfair
I am not you; I am me
Who else would I want to be?

Not a disability
Unpredictability
Many definitions though
For each stage in life we grow.

The Stages of Life

Autism is not a word
Has this thought ever occurred?
Autism is a lifetime
A ladder that we must climb.

From the moment we're conceived
Who would have thought or believed
The trials and the achievements
As we climb over the fence.

The tiny foetus that has hope
How hard they will learn to cope
Stage by stage making progress
Learning ways which to express.

Throughout the stages we grow
Sometimes you see a slight glow
Almost as if a hurdle
Has become surmountable.

Keep your focus on each goal
Even though it may seem small
Along life's path you will find
Many experiences lined.

Parents' 50th Anniversary

Lightning Source UK Ltd.
Milton Keynes UK
UKHW052014280119
336214UK00009B/166/P